Contents

Any words appearing in the text in bold, **like this**, are explained in the Glossary.

What is a hamster?

Hamsters are one of the most popular types of small pet. These lovable creatures live in homes around the world. People have been keeping cats for thousands of years, but hamsters have only been kept as pets for around 60 years.

In the wild

Wild hamsters live in **burrows** in dry places such as **deserts** where few plants can grow. The seeds and other plant foods that wild hamsters eat are found around a wide area. When they find food, hamsters eat as much as they can, and carry more back to their burrows. Hamsters store food in their burrows to eat later.

Wild Syrian hamsters are now rare in the deserts of the Middle East where they were first discovered.

What's in a name?

The name "hamster" comes from the German word "hamstern", which means "hoard" or "store". The hamster got its name because of its habit of storing or hoarding food!

Keeping Pets

Hamsters

Louise and Richard Spilsbury

www.heinemann.co.uk/library
Visit our website to find out more information about Heinemann Library books.

To order:
☎ Phone 44 (0) 1865 888066
🖹 Send a fax to 44 (0) 1865 314091
🖥 Visit the Heinemann bookshop at www.heinemann.co.uk/library to browse our catalogue and order online.

First published in Great Britain by Heinemann Library, Halley Court, Jordan Hill, Oxford OX2 8EJ, part of Harcourt Education.

Heinemann is a registered trademark of Harcourt Education Ltd.

Editorial: Andrew Farrow and Stig Vatland
Design: Richard Parker and Q2A Solutions
Picture Research: Maria Joannou and Catherine Bevan
Production: Chloe Bloom

Originated by Modern Age Repro
Printed and Bound in China
by South China Printing Company

The paper used to print this book comes from sustainable resources.

10 digit ISBN: 0 431 12428 0 (hardback)
13 digit ISBN: 978 0 431 12428 5

10 digit ISBN: 0 431 12455 8 (paperback)
13 digit ISBN: 978 0 431 12455 1

11 10 09 08 07
10 9 8 7 6 5 4 3 2 1

British Library Cataloguing in Publication Data
Spilsbury, Louise and Richard
Hamsters. - (Keeping pets)
1.Hamsters as pets - Juvenile literature
636.9'356
A full catalogue record for this book is available from the British Library.

Acknowledgements
The publishers would like to thank the following for permission to reproduce photographs: Acorn Stock Images pp. **4**, **8 top**, **8 bottom**, **9**, **22 bottom**; Alamy Images p. **17** (Maximilian Weinzierl); Ardea p. **7 bottom**; Armitage Pet Care p. **19 top**; Dave Bradford p. **43**; Harcourt Education Ltd (Haddon Davies) p. **25 bottom**; Harcourt Education Ltd (Tudor Photography) pp. **5**, **6**, **7 top**, **10**, **11**, **13 bottom**, **14**, **15**, **16**, **18**, **19 bottom**, **20**, **22 top**, **23**, **24**, **25 top**, **26**, **27 top**, **27 bottom**, **28**, **29 top**, **29 bottom**, **30**, **31 top**, **32 top**, **32 bottom**, **33**, **34 top**, **34 bottom**, **35**, **36 left**, **36 right**, **38 bottom**, **40**, **41 top**, **45 middle left**, **45 middle right**, **45 bottom**, **45 top**; Robyn Bright pp. **13 top**, **21**, **31 bottom**, **37**, **38 top**, **39**, **41 bottom**, **42**.

Need to know

- When you keep any pet, it is your responsibility to always look after it. For example, that means giving it enough food and water, and helping to keep it clean and healthy.
- There are laws in many countries to protect pet hamsters from cruelty.

History of pet hamsters

In the 1930s, a scientist captured four wild hamsters in Syria. Some **descendants** of these four hamsters were taken to live in zoos and university laboratories. People soon learnt that these Syrian hamsters were easy to keep, and the first pet hamsters went on sale in 1945. Over time, people bred hamsters of different colours. People also started to keep other types of hamster from different countries as pets.

Pet hamsters live happy, healthy lives when they are looked after properly.

5

Hamster facts

Hamsters belong to a group of animals called **mammals**. Like other mammals, including dogs and people, hamsters have hair on their bodies. Female mammals can **suckle** (feed) their young with milk from their own bodies. Hamsters seem nothing like bigger mammals such as whales, but they have many things in common with mice and rats. That is because hamsters, mice, and rats are all **rodents**.

Rodent teeth

All rodents have similar teeth. They have four long, curved, yellowish teeth called **incisors** – two at the top and two at the bottom. A rodent's incisors keep growing throughout its life, so it always has long, sharp teeth to eat with. The tips of the incisors are worn down as rodents **gnaw** on hard food such as nuts, so the teeth do not get overgrown.

If hamsters cannot gnaw, their teeth keep growing longer and longer.

Pouches

Hamsters, like some other rodents, have **pouches** in their cheeks. The pouches are folds of stretchy skin that reach from their lips to their shoulders. Hamsters use their pouches to carry food and bedding material back to their **burrows**.

Hamster babies

Most female rodents have lots of babies. Syrian hamsters usually have about 8 babies, but some have as many as 26! Each newborn baby weighs about the same as a teaspoon of flour. The babies suckle for about three weeks and then eat adult food. Hamsters can have their own babies from about five weeks old!

When full, the pouches on a Syrian hamster make its head look twice as wide!

Did you know?

Hamsters are **nocturnal**. That means they are active at night and usually sleep during the day. In the wild, this way of living means they avoid the hot sunshine in the day and search for food at night when it is cool. Hamsters use their senses of hearing and smell to find their way around in the dark.

Newborn hamsters have no hair and their eyes are closed. After about 10 days, their eyelids open and they have grown hair.

7

Syrian hamsters

The hamster that most people keep as a pet is the Syrian hamster (see picture at top of page 7). Syrian hamsters have a stocky body with a very short tail. Some people think they look a bit like little bears. The Syrian hamster is often called a golden hamster. This is because wild Syrian hamsters usually have golden brown backs, a white belly, and dark cheek patches. But pet Syrian hamsters can be a different colour to wild hamsters. For example, some are dark grey instead of golden brown, but with similar white and dark patches. Other Syrian hamsters are just one colour, such as black, all over their bodies.

Hair

Syrian hamsters have different types of hair. Some have long fluffy hair and some have short hair. One rare **breed** of Syrian hamster is completely hairless!

Russian hamsters normally have hairy feet! In the wild, the hair helps keep their feet warm.

Chinese hamsters usually have a dark stripe running down their back.

8

Other types of hamster

There are three other types of hamster that some people keep as pets. They are all smaller than the Syrian hamster, and they are all slightly different to each other. Russian and Chinese hamsters are about half the length of Syrian hamsters. They also look quite different. Russian hamsters have a small, rounded body and a very short tail. Chinese hamsters have a thin, mouse-shaped body with a long tail. Both of these hamsters come in a range of colours. One type of Russian hamster is called the "winter white" because of its pure white hair.

The final type of hamster is called the Roborovski hamster. This is by far the smallest kind. Adult Roborovski hamsters are only around 5 centimetres (2 inches) long. Many are sandy coloured and have white eyebrows.

Roborovski hamsters are a quarter of the size of the Syrian hamster and can move much more quickly.

Did you know?

- Hamsters live for around two or two-and-a-half years.
- Hamsters grow to about 15–20 centimetres (6–7 inches) long.
- Adult hamsters weigh about 180–200 grams (6–8 ounces).
- Hamsters have four toes on each of their front feet and five toes on each of their back feet.

9

Are hamsters for you?

Hamsters make good pets for many people of all ages. A lot of people choose them just because they look cute and they are fascinating to watch. But there are a lot of things to think about when choosing the right kind of pet for you. Here are some good and not-so-good points about hamsters. You should think about these points carefully. Most people choose a Syrian hamster when they get their first one, so the information here is all about this type of hamster.

Hamster good points

- Hamsters sleep during the day when you are usually at school, and are active later in the day when you are around.
- Hamsters are cheap to feed. Equipment, such as a cage, is usually inexpensive, too.
- Hamsters generally do not smell as much as some other **rodents**, such as mice.
- They do not take up much space, so they are ideal if you live in a flat or a small house.
- There are a lot of different hair colours to choose from.

It feels very special to make friends with your pet hamster. There are moments when your hamster seems just as interested in you as you are in him.

Hamster not-so-good points

- Hamsters can bite you. They rely on smell to find food, so if your fingers smell of food, they might bite your fingers. They may also bite if you wake them up.
- Hamsters will **gnaw** and chew things in your house. They can cause a lot of damage with their tough **incisors**.
- Because they are **nocturnal**, hamsters might make a lot of noise at night when you are trying to sleep.
- Hamsters do not live for very long.
- Some hamsters do not like being handled.

Hamsters can fit in with your life fairly easily. You might even have a quiet, safe corner of your bedroom where a hamster cage could fit.

Yes or no?

Have you thought carefully about all the good and bad points about living with a pet hamster? Are you ready to clean out a cage regularly and to give your hamster food and water every day, no matter what else you have to do? If the answer to these questions is yes, then it's time to choose your hamster!

Choosing your hamster

When you are sure you want to keep a hamster, you need to make sure your parents or guardians are happy about it, too. After all, they will need to help you to look after it sometimes. They will help you buy the food and equipment that you need. They should also help you choose your hamster.

What type of hamster?

Most pet experts recommend Syrian hamsters for children. This is mostly because they are the biggest and the easiest to handle. They are also less likely to get scared or bite you when you are learning to handle them.

The smaller types of hamster do not make great pets for young people, mainly because they are difficult to handle.

- Russian hamsters bite more than the other types, especially if they are not handled properly.
- Roborovski hamsters are so fast moving and active that it is difficult to catch them.
- Chinese hamsters are nervous, so they are not always easy to catch safely when you want to handle them.

Top tip
All of the small types of hamster need to be kept in cages they cannot escape from. The bars should be very close together so the hamsters cannot squeeze through them and escape.

How many hamsters?

Adult Syrian hamsters like to live alone. Syrian hamster babies can live happily together up to the age of two months. Then they start to fight and can injure each other. In the wild, a Syrian hamster will attack another hamster it meets. This is especially true if the other hamster goes near a **burrow** where its own food is stored. If you choose a Syrian hamster for a pet, it will need its own cage.

Roborovski and Russian hamsters are usually happier living with other hamsters of their own kind. However, if you see any signs of fighting between hamsters in the same cage, you will have to separate them.

Roborovski hamsters are usually happy living in small groups.

If you want to keep several Syrian hamsters, you will need to keep them in separate cages.

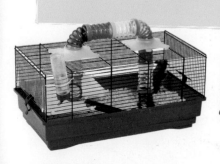

Top tip

If you think your Syrian hamster is lonely or bored, never get another hamster to keep her company. Instead, try to make your pet's life more interesting by providing a new toy or spending more time with her.

Male or female?

Both male and female hamsters make good pets, but different hamsters behave differently, just like people. Many people say that male hamsters are generally more relaxed and even-tempered than females. They are also more tolerant of handling. Sometimes adult females smell more than usual, but the smell usually goes away after a while.

Top tip

It is very tricky to tell whether a hamster is male or female. The only obvious difference is that males are sometimes bigger. It is best to check with the person you get your pet hamster from. They probably know much more about hamsters than you do, and can tell the difference.

How old?

People usually get their pet hamster when it is young. Young hamsters can get used to proper handling a little better than older hamsters. You should get your hamster when it is aged six weeks or older. If you choose a female, make sure she has been kept separately from males. Remember that young female hamsters can become pregnant from five weeks old.

Hamsters should not be taken away from their mothers before they are six weeks old, because they may not be able to feed themselves properly.

Breeding

Vets say that you should never let adult male and female hamsters live in the same cage because they might **breed**. There are two main reasons why this is a problem.
- It is very difficult to find homes for young hamsters.
- It is very expensive to care for a lot of hamsters properly. For example, it costs a lot of money to buy cages to house the hamsters separately and to pay vet and food bills.

So if you plan to keep more than one of the smaller types of hamster together, make sure they are all girls or all boys. Otherwise you will find yourself with more hamsters than you can look after!

You may see young hamsters together in a pet shop, but males should be separated from females at 3 to 4 weeks old so that they do not breed.

Where to find a pet hamster

When you get your pet hamster, you will want to know if it is male or female. If it is a female, you will want to know that it has been kept separately from males so you can be sure it is not pregnant. Only get a hamster from a place where the people can tell you all about the animal. If they cannot give you the information you need, go to another place to choose a hamster.

Some people get their hamsters from private **breeders** or **rescue homes**. Private breeders carefully breed hamsters with particular colours. They also record a lot of information about all their hamsters. Breeders know who their hamsters' parents are and when they were born. That means you will know a lot about the hamster you choose. Private breeders often handle their hamsters, which will make it easier for you to handle them, too.

It is a good sign that a hamster is alert and active. This is difficult to tell if you go to choose your hamster when it is asleep!

What to look for

Wherever you get it from, you will want to choose a healthy hamster. Healthy hamsters are **alert** and interested in everything. Their cages should be clean with plenty of food and water. There should also be a lot of space for them.

Health clues

It is difficult to know for sure if a hamster is ill, but here are five clues:

- it has a thin body, with the outline of its bones showing
- it is sleepy or very slow-moving when others are awake
- it has runny or sticky eyes
- it has a wet or dirty bottom
- it has matted or patchy hair.

Even if the hamster you want to choose looks well, look at the other hamsters in the same place. If one is sick, then others may develop the same illness.

Hamsters from rescue homes or **shelters** often need more love and care because they have not been cared for properly by their previous owners.

What do I need?

Before you bring your hamster home you need to make sure you have everything he will need. The most important thing is somewhere to live, usually a cage or other enclosed home. You will also need things such as a wheel and toys to put inside the cage.

Hamsters should be kept in as big a cage as possible, so they have a lot of space.

Wire cages

Wire cages for hamsters have a top and sides made of wire, sometimes coloured, that fits onto a plastic tray base. Some wire cages have one or two extra wire shelves inside for the hamster to climb onto. A deep base stops bedding and other material from spilling out of the cage. Wire cages are a good choice because hamsters enjoy climbing up the bars, they let in lots of air, and they are easy to clean. The problem is that they are not **draught proof**.

Wire cage sizes

- Experts recommend a cage size of 75 centimetres (30 inches) long and 30 centimetres (12 inches) wide, so there is enough room for the hamster to move around.
- A cage should be tall enough to easily fit in an exercise wheel.
- Russian, Chinese, and Roborovski hamsters are small enough to squeeze through the bars of a cage if the gaps are bigger than half-a-centimetre (0.2 inches)!

Plastic hamster homes

Many people keep smaller types of hamster in special plastic homes. These are usually too small for a Syrian hamster. Plastic homes are made of solid plastic compartments and tunnels that clip together. The hamster home should have one small compartment for the hamster to sleep in and a much larger one for it to live in and explore. Plastic homes are draught proof, but have to be taken apart for cleaning.

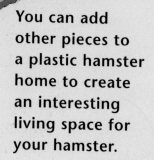

Other homes

Some people keep hamsters in **aquariums** or wooden cages. Aquariums are made of thick glass or plastic, and should have a strong wire mesh lid. Aquariums are often heavy, which makes them difficult to lift and clean. Cages made from wood and wire mesh do not make good hamster homes. Wood soaks up **urine** and gets smelly. It is also gradually chewed away by the hamster.

You can add other pieces to a plastic hamster home to create an interesting living space for your hamster.

A lid on an aquarium stops hamsters escaping, stops other pets harming them, and makes sure nothing gets dropped on them.

Where should the cage go?

It is important to place your hamster's cage somewhere safe. It needs to be on a wide, strong surface so it cannot fall off and harm the hamster inside. It needs to be in a quiet place so noise does not frighten the hamster. It needs to be out of draughts and away from sunny windows and central heating radiators. Hamsters can get sick if they get too cold or hot. You might like to have the hamster cage in your bedroom, but remember that hamsters are active all through the night and may disturb your sleep!

Flooring

All cages need to have a clean layer of flooring material in the bottom. This is to make the floor comfortable for your hamster to move around on and to soak up **urine**. It is cheapest to buy wood shavings. However, hamsters are **allergic** to the chemicals in some types of wood, such as cedar, especially when the wood gets wet with urine. It is safest to buy shavings or small animal litter from a pet shop. Different animal litters are made of safe wood or recycled paper.

Put a layer of litter about 2.5 centimetres (1 inch) thick in the base of the hamster's cage or living compartment.

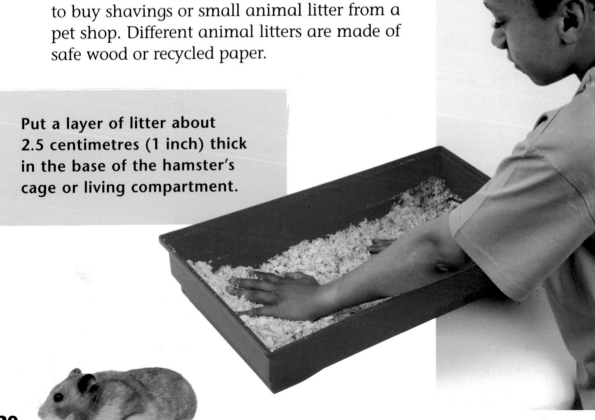

Bedding

Hamsters need a comfortable small space to sleep in. This can be a separate chamber in a plastic cage or a short cardboard tube or box in a wire cage or **aquarium**. Fill the bedroom with soft bedding material so your hamster can make a nest. Check the table below to see what material is safe to use.

Hamsters sleep for around 14 hours each day.

Bedding type	Yes or no	Why?
Cotton wool	No	It is harmful if the hamster eats it. The fine fibres can get caught around a hamster's legs, causing injury
Straw	No	Sharp edges can injure the insides of a hamster's **pouches**
Shredded newspaper	No	Printing ink may make a hamster ill
Hay	Yes/No	Only use hay if it is clean and not **mouldy** or dusty
Shredded toilet paper or kitchen towel	Yes	Make sure it is unperfumed, and white

Wheels

Hamsters are active animals. Wild hamsters can run up to 8 kilometres (5 miles) a night in search of food! You cannot have an enormous cage, but you can help your hamster exercise by giving it a wheel to run around in. The wheel you choose should be made of solid plastic, not wire. Hamsters can get their legs and heads trapped in wire wheels. The wheel needs to be fixed firmly in the cage so it does not fall over when your hamster uses it.

The hamster wheel you choose should be big enough for your hamster to use comfortably without arching (curving) its back.

Having a ball

A hamster ball is a clear plastic ball that you can put a hamster in. As the hamster runs, it rolls the ball around. Some hamsters like these for exercise, but others can become frightened. If you plan to use a ball, let your hamster explore the opened ball and get used to it before you shut it in for the first time. Also, check that the ball is big enough for your hamster to move comfortably inside. Only ever let a hamster use the ball for 15 minutes or less.

Always watch a hamster in a ball carefully so that it doesn't roll somewhere dangerous, such as through an open door or down stairs.

Other hamster toys

Toys are important because they stop your hamster getting bored. There are a lot of toys you can buy from pet shops, such as plastic houses, seesaws, or wooden climbing blocks. However, hamsters also like to play with things you might already have in your home. These include empty cardboard egg boxes, tubes, ping-pong balls or pieces of thick, knotted rope. Hamsters will shred some of these things, so you will have to replace them!

Top tip
Remember that your hamster will want some space to move around in its cage. Do not overfill the cage with toys.

Toys can be swapped around now and again. This means your hamster will not get bored with the same things all the time.

Looking after your hamster

You must look after your hamster properly by giving it enough food and water, making sure its cage is clean, and that it is healthy.

Hamster mix

The main food that hamsters eat is hamster mix. This is a mixture of peanuts, barley, oats, and sunflower seeds. There are special food mixes for other small pets, but they do not all provide the **nutrients** a hamster needs. Hamsters usually eat about a tablespoon of fresh hamster mix each day. Some hamsters eat less than this because they are fussy eaters. However, an empty bowl does not mean your hamster needs more food. It may just be storing food somewhere in its cage!

Fresh food

Hamsters need variety in their diet so they need fresh fruit and vegetables at least once a week. Try giving your pet carrot, apple, courgette, celery, cauliflower, melon, parsley, grapes, and grass. Be careful not to give too much cabbage and other green vegetables as they can give your hamster an upset stomach.

Check with your pet shop whether a food mix is suitable for hamsters before you feed it to your pet.

Feeding tips!

- Feed your pet hamster when he wakes up.
- You can put hamster mix in a china or metal bowl. These are easy to clean and the hamster cannot chew them like he can a plastic bowl. You can also sprinkle dry food on the cage floor or hide pieces around the cage. This is more like the way hamsters find food in the wild.
- Try giving your hamster pieces of fresh food from your fingers. If you drop them on the cage floor or leave them in a bowl, they can go **mouldy** and get covered in bedding material.

Give a small piece of fresh food, about a centimetre (half-an-inch) cubed, at a time.

Water supply

Hamsters must always have a supply of fresh water. A plastic water bottle from a pet shop is better than a bowl because it cannot be knocked over or get dirty. Secure the bottle to the outside of the cage. It should have a metal spout with a ball at the end where the water comes out. Always keep it filled up with water, especially in warm weather when most animals drink more than usual.

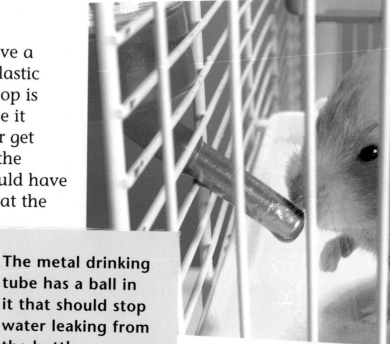

The metal drinking tube has a ball in it that should stop water leaking from the bottle.

Foods to avoid

There are some types of food that you should never give to your hamster. This is because they can make him ill. Sticky foods such as sweets and chocolate easily get stuck in a hamster's cheek **pouches** and can cause damage. Pieces of citrus fruit such as oranges can upset a hamster's delicate stomach. Some foods can cause more serious illness. These include raw potato, onion, raw kidney beans, flower bulbs, buttercups, and oak leaves.

Top tip

If you are unsure what fresh food is safe for your hamster, ask someone who knows. You could try asking an adult you live with, a vet, or someone who works at a pet shop.

You should never give your hamster any of these foods because they could make him ill.

Food treats

Just like people, hamsters like food treats. Hamster treats bought from pet shops are often sweet. Too many of these can damage a hamster's teeth or make your pet fat and unhealthy. Instead, offer your hamster tiny pieces of brazil nut, cheese, soft toast, hard-boiled egg, cooked pasta, or currants. You will soon find out what your hamster likes best.

Chewing

Hamsters will **gnaw** on anything they can find to keep their **incisors** the right length. They like to chew cardboard boxes and even plastic tubes. You should provide hard things for your hamster to gnaw on. Blocks of fruit wood or dog biscuits are suitable, but do not give your pet soft wood or the stones (big seeds) from inside fruit. These can break into sharp pieces that will scratch the insides of your hamster's cheek pouches.

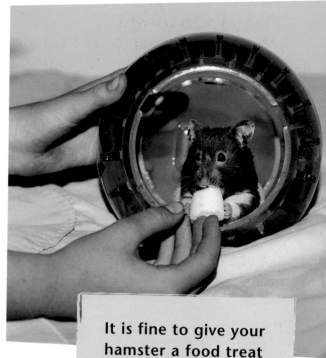

It is fine to give your hamster a food treat once in a while, but not every day.

Gnawing on chewy snacks is good for your hamster's teeth.

Top tip

Sometimes hamsters chew on wire cage bars, which can damage their teeth. Chewing bars is usually a sign that the hamster is bored. If your hamster does this, try to make his life more fun by providing different toys for him to play with.

Daily cleaning

An important part of looking after your hamster is keeping her cage clean. You need to do a couple of easy cleaning jobs every day. First, take your hamster out of the cage and put her somewhere safe (see page 35 for ideas). Remove and replace any uneaten fresh food from the floor or nest area, before it goes **mouldy**. Scoop out the wood shavings from the damp toilet corner and replace them with fresh ones. Finally, change the drinking water and fill up the food bowl.

Do not forget to wear gloves when you clean out your hamster's cage. Always wash your hands after holding your hamster and after cleaning out her cage.

Weekly washing

Once a week, you need to clean the whole cage. Put your pet somewhere safe, away from the cleaning area. Take the cage apart and wash all the parts of the cage with warm soapy water or a special **disinfectant** cleaner from a pet shop. It is also a good idea to wash the bowl, bottle, and plastic toys. Then rinse all the pieces with clean, warm water. Make sure it is all completely dry before you put the cage back together and put in fresh flooring material.

Clean hamsters

Hamsters **groom** themselves to keep their fur clean and healthy. If your hamster smells, it is because you are not cleaning her cage often enough, not because she is dirty. Never try to bathe or wash your hamster because they are scared of water. They could get chilled and catch a cold. In the wild, hamsters sometimes roll in sand to keep clean. You could take your hamster out of her cage and put her into a tray of sand that pet shops sell for pet chinchillas. Hamsters like to roll around in this. (Always use sand. Never use the dust that pet shops also sell for chinchillas.)

Hamsters are very clean animals and often groom themselves.

Top tip

Smells are very important to hamsters. They feel happier when their cage smells familiar.

- When you put the nest back into the cage, make sure some of the clean old bedding material is in there, too.
- If there is some dried food in the nest, leave a bit there. This is the hamster's food store and she will be upset if you take it all away.

Long-haired hamsters

Long-haired hamsters groom themselves to keep clean. You should brush them once a week with a toothbrush to help them remove dirt and wood shavings from their fur.

Most long-haired hamsters enjoy having their fur brushed.

Happy and healthy?

An important part of caring for your hamster is keeping an eye on her health. This is not hard to do. Once you get to know your hamster, you will soon spot any changes in the way she moves, feeds, or plays. Then you will know when something is wrong. Hamsters are small and can become very ill quite quickly. If you notice a change, take your hamster to the vet for a check-up straight away.

Check it out

When you stroke or handle your hamster, feel her all over to check if she has any lumps, bumps, or cuts. Check that her fur feels smooth, clean, and soft. When you feed her, check that she is eating her usual amount. When you clean the cage, check that her **faeces** (droppings) look normal.

Things to look out for

Here are some things to look out for:

- Does your hamster feel lighter or heavier than usual? A change in weight can mean a hamster has a health problem.
- Is your hamster limping or moving awkwardly? She may have injured a leg or be ill.
- Are your hamster's ears, eyes, nose, and tail clean? If these are dirty or runny, your hamster could be ill.

Normal hamster faeces (droppings) should look like this. If they are very runny or too hard, your hamster might be sick.

Hibernation

If Syrian hamsters get too cold, they **hibernate**. In the wild, animals hibernate to survive cold winters when there is not much food around. They find somewhere safe and go into a very deep sleep. If your hamster hibernates, she may be so still and quiet that you think she is dead. Do not panic. Look closely and you will see her whiskers twitch now and then.

When you watch your hamster play, you will notice if there is something wrong or if she moves differently.

If your hamster hibernates, you will still be able to see her whiskers moving as she breathes.

Out of hibernation

If your hamster hibernates, you will need to warm her up to wake her up. Move the cage to a warm place. Keep things quiet and calm until she has woken up, and then offer her some food and water.

Handling your hamster

Most hamsters really enjoy being handled. However, they may take a while to get used to being held, so be patient! A few hamsters never enjoy being handled, but it is still lots of fun to watch them play.

First steps

Before your hamster is ready to be handled, he will need to get used to your touch. Start by stroking him gently with a finger while he is safe in his cage. Talk gently to him as well. Then try stroking him with your hand.

When your hamster is used to being stroked, offer him your hand with a piece of food in the middle of it. The hamster may climb onto your hand to get the food. Do not grab him. Just let him explore you.

A hamster needs to know your smell and touch before he will be happy about being handled.

Once he has got to know you, your hamster will be happy to walk onto your hand.

Picking up your hamster

When your hamster is used to the touch of your hands, then he is ready to be handled. First, take off the top of the cage or open the doors, and slowly put both hands in. Cup your hands together and gently scoop up the hamster.

Handling bites

- Hamsters bite when they are frightened or do not feel safe. They often bite if you pick them up suddenly, especially if they are asleep. Only handle your hamster when he is awake.
- Hamsters may also bite if they are upset. A sure sign that your hamster is not happy is if he makes a noisy chattering sound.

When you scoop up your hamster, keep your hands slightly open so the hamster does not feel trapped.

Lifting by the scruff

You may have seen people lifting a hamster by the scruff of its neck. Vets sometimes do this so they can easily examine underneath. However, lifting by the scruff is best left to experts. They know how to do it properly without hurting the animal.

Hand to hand

To get your hamster to walk from one hand to the other, first scoop him up and close your fingers around him so he can feel them. If he tries to jump, let him. Never hold on tight to stop him from jumping as this may frighten him and make him bite. Soon he will be happy to walk from hand to hand and enjoy being stroked while being held.

Hamsters enjoy climbing between your hands.

Once your hamster gets used to you, he will feel safe when you hold him.

Care when handling

Always handle your hamster close to the ground. This is because hamsters often try to jump out of your hands when you lift them. If a hamster falls a long way to the ground, it can be badly injured. Hamsters are less likely to jump if they are face to face with you when you lift them.

Exploring a playpen

When you know how to pick up and handle your hamster, give him a chance to explore an out-of-cage area. This can be a hamster playpen bought from a pet shop, or a large, deep, strong cardboard box. Whatever the space you provide, it should be escape-proof and safe. There should be nothing dangerous for your hamster to chew, such as electrical wires or poisonous house plants. There should be no holes in floorboards that he could disappear into. There should be no pets around that could harm him, such as a cat. Never put him on a table. Hamsters have poor eyesight and he may fall off the edge.

It is great fun watching a hamster explore. You can invent new challenges for your pet in his cage, such as runs and mazes, made out of tubes and rolls. Try hiding bits of food behind toys to see if your hamster can sniff them out!

Hamsters love to investigate new places and things.

What to do if a hamster escapes

- Close all the doors and windows in your home.
- If you are not sure which room he is in, put a bowl of food in each room before you go to bed. Check which one has less food in it when you wake up.
- Move the cage or just the wheel to the room with the empty bowl. The hamster will probably soon be back to sniff round his home all by himself.
- Move in quietly and gently scoop him up!

Health matters

The chances are that your hamster will be healthy and happy and hardly ever get ill. But you are responsible for your pet, so you need to keep an eye out for any signs of illness. If you are ever worried about your pet's health, tell an adult right away. Here are some of the health problems your hamster might experience. If you do not know what is wrong with your pet, take her to the vet.

Colds

Does your hamster sneeze or have a runny nose? Does she move less and more slowly than usual? Does she have wheezy breathing?

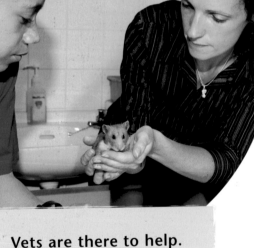

Vets are there to help. They are trained to be gentle when they examine your pet.

You do not want to pass your cold on to your pets, so wash your hands before handling your hamster.

If the answer to any of these questions is yes, your hamster probably has a cold. The important thing to do is to keep her warm and give her plenty of food. Keep an eye on your pet, and if she is still ill after a couple of days, go to the vet. If left too long, colds can turn into **pneumonia**, which is much more serious. Vets can give your hamster an **antibiotic injection** to treat pneumonia.

Top tip

Hamsters can catch colds and flu from people. If you have a cold, handle your hamster less often, and then only do so after you have carefully washed your hands.

Eye problems

There are several reasons why your hamster's eyes might start to look red and sore, or a bit runny or stuck closed. Sometimes dusty bedding causes eye problems, so clean the bedding or change the type you use. Breathing problems or simply old age can also cause sore eyes, so if it does not clear up, ask a vet for advice. The vet may give you an antibiotic ointment to put on the eye.

If a hamster's eyes are all gummy and stuck together, you can bathe them with cotton wool dipped in cooled, boiled water. Ask an adult to boil and cool the water for you.

Teeth troubles

A hamster's **incisors** go on growing throughout its life. To keep its front teeth the right length, a hamster needs to chew on something hard. If **rodent** teeth are not worn down ·properly, they can grow too long. Vets can clip hamster teeth using special clippers. Then you should give your hamster a hardwood block to **gnaw** on so it does not happen again.

Hamsters find it hard or even impossible to eat when they have overgrown teeth. Sometimes long teeth like this can break off.

Your hamster may not like having her teeth clipped, but it does not hurt her. She will be much more comfortable after it is done.

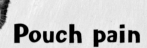

Pouch pain

A splinter of wood or piece of sharp food can damage the lining in a hamster's cheek **pouches**. Sometimes food can get stuck inside a pouch and cause discomfort. You will need to see a vet to take care of pouch problems like this.

Claws

Hamsters can also suffer from overgrown claws. If your hamster's claws get too long, they can catch more easily on bedding or cage bars and get damaged. If the nails break, the toes can become infected. If you notice that your hamster's claws are getting long, ask your vet to clip them.

Fur loss

It is natural for hamsters to lose some of their hair twice a year. This is called **moulting**. Their thick winter coat of fur drops out as it gets warmer and is replaced by a thinner summer coat. Then in autumn, the thinner coat drops out to be replaced by another thick winter coat. Sometimes moulting can leave your hamster with bald patches. Don't worry – the fur should grow back within a couple of weeks.

Mites

Hamsters can also lose fur because of mites. Mites are tiny insects that live on animal skin. They can make hamster skin so sore and red that hair falls out. It is easy to get rid of mites by treating your hamster with a special spray or shampoo from the vet or a pet shop.

Top tip

When your hamster starts to lose fur, check her skin. If the skin is flaky, scabby, or sore, it may mean that the fur loss is caused by something other than moulting. Take your hamster to the vet for a check-up to find out.

After you have treated your hamster for mites, change all the bedding and flooring, and clean the cage to get rid of any other mites.

Tummy troubles

If your hamster has very runny **faeces** (droppings) and his body looks a bit thin and sunken, he has **diarrhoea**. Hamsters may get diarrhoea if they eat too much fruit or too many vegetables, or if they have too many treat foods. Diarrhoea makes hamsters unwell because they lose too much water and become **dehydrated**.

To cure diarrhoea, stop feeding your hamster fresh foods and make sure he drinks plenty of water. If your pet still has diarrhoea after a couple of days, ask your vet for advice. The vet may suggest giving your hamster a teaspoon of arrowroot powder mixed to a paste with a little water.

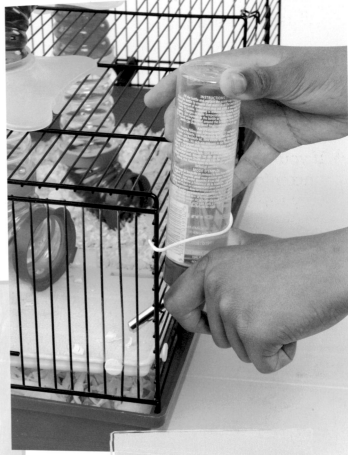

Over-heating

Hamsters can get over-heated fairly easily. When a hamster is too hot, he breathes quickly and heavily and moves slowly. Move him to a cooler spot and give him plenty of water to drink.

If your hamster has diarrhoea, it is very important to make sure he drinks plenty of water.

Wounds

If a hamster damages his claws or cuts his skin, soak up any blood with a tissue and then bathe the area with an **antiseptic** lotion. Keep the cage and nest very clean to prevent **infection**. If a wound is slow to heal, see a vet.

Wet tail

If your hamster looks very tired and uncomfortable, stops eating, and has very runny faeces, he may have "wet tail". Wet tail is a serious disease, so take your hamster to a vet immediately. The vet will treat your hamster with medicine, but the chances of surviving are not good. Wet tail can spread easily to other pets, so clean the cage and toys carefully and keep a close eye on any other hamsters.

Clean a hamster's wounds very gently.

This hamster shows signs of wet tail, so he should be taken straight to a vet.

41

Growing old

It is normal for any pet to change as it gets older. Hamsters may start to show some signs of old age from when they are just one year old.

Health checks are more important than ever because older hamsters can get sick even more quickly than younger ones. However, many older hamsters enjoy good health until the end of their lives. They will probably want to play less, but many still enjoy being handled.

Elderly hamsters can look a bit scruffy because they find it more difficult to **groom** themselves.

Signs of ageing in hamsters

- Your hamster might start to lose some hair, so his coat will begin to look patchy and his skin will look drier.
- He might weigh less and sleep more of the time.
- He will be less **agile** and move more slowly around his cage.
- He may get sick more easily if it gets cold. He may be happier if his cage is in a warmer place.
- His teeth may become brittle and break easily. It is best to give soft food such as hamster mix softened in water.

Coming to the end

Like other **rodents**, hamsters do not live for very long. Many old hamsters die in their sleep. Others get ill and never recover. Sometimes old hamsters get so ill that they are uncomfortable when you handle them. They are not enjoying life any more. This may be the time to take the hamster to the vet to end its life. Putting a pet to sleep is when a vet gives a special **injection** or gas to an animal to stop it breathing. This is a painless, gentle way to stop an animal suffering.

Top tip

It helps a lot of pet owners to bury their pet when it dies. It gives them a chance to say goodbye and think about the pet's life.

Losing a friend

Whether your pet hamster dies naturally or with the help of a vet, you will be very sad. You will probably feel like crying and you will miss your little friend. Do not worry, it is completely natural to feel like this. In time you will start to feel better and less sad when you remember your pet.

Burying your pet can help you to remember him.

Keeping a record

The time you spend with your pet is very rewarding. It is easiest to remember what you have done together if you make a record of your hamster's life.

Hamster scrapbook

A hamster scrapbook is a good place to keep a lot of different types of information about your hamster. For example, details of where you got her, what kind of hamster she is, what her favourite foods are, when she has been ill, and what toys she enjoys best. Stick in photos or drawings of her to make it look good. Remember to write captions for your pictures so you can remember what they show.

Knowing more

You can learn a lot about hamsters by keeping one as a pet. You can also learn a lot about them in other ways. Here are some ways to find out more:

* Talk to friends who also keep hamsters.
* Read other books about hamsters.
* Test your hamster with different tasks, such as finding food or mazes.
* Visit zoos or wildlife parks where hamsters and other **nocturnal rodents** live.
* Visit websites of hamster **breeders**. You will find out lots about other pet hamsters.
* Visit pet shows where different hamsters are on show and where you might meet other hamster enthusiasts.

Top tip

Some people put their hamster information on a family website rather than in a scrapbook. You could ask an adult to help you do this.

Top hamster! You will be amazed at all the different types of hamster on display at a pet show.

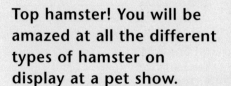

When you make your scrapbook, you could include pictures of you and your hamster.

In your scrapbook, you could include a picture from the day your hamster arrived at your house.

It is a good idea to write labels for your pictures and include the dates they were taken.

Glossary

agile   able to move quickly and easily

alert   lively and interested in everything

allergic   if an animal is allergic to something, this means it can make it sick

antibiotic   medicine that can cure some animal diseases

antiseptic   something that stops germs from growing

aquarium   tank made from see-through glass or plastic with an open top

breed   type of animal. Also, when animals have babies together.

breeder   someone who raises a particular kind of animal. A hamster breeder keeps hamsters so he or she can sell their babies.

burrow   hole in the ground which an animal lives or sleeps in

dehydrated   when an animal does not have enough water in its body. Almost all animals need to drink water every day to stay healthy.

descendants   generation of animal that comes after another. You are a descendant of your grandparents and great-grandparents.

deserts   dry, sandy, and rocky areas of land in very hot places

diarrhoea   runny faeces

disinfectant   spray or liquid that destroys germs

draught proof   describes something that stops cold draughts of air from blowing through

faeces   droppings or poo

gnaw   chew or bite

groom   to clean an animal's fur. Many animals groom themselves.

hibernate   when an animal goes into a deep, long sleep, usually to survive a season when it is very cold or hard for it to find food

incisors   long front teeth

infection   illness

injection   when a needle is used to put medicine into an animal's body

mammal   animal with hair or fur that can feed its babies on milk from its own body

mouldy   rotten

moult   when an animal's fur drops out to be replaced by a new coat

nocturnal   active at night and asleep in the daytime

nutrients   parts of food that an animal's body needs to grow and stay healthy

pneumonia   illness where the lungs become infected and full of a liquid called pus

pouches   floppy folds of stretchy skin inside a hamster's cheeks

rescue homes   places where abandoned pets are cared for until they find a new home

rodent   animal with strong front teeth that keep growing throughout its life

shelters   places where abandoned pets are cared for until they find a new home

suckle   when a baby mammal drinks milk from its mother's body

urine   wee, a waste liquid that comes from an animal's body

Further reading

Care for Your Hamster (RSPCA Pet Guides), (Collins, 2005)

How to Look After Your Hamster, Colin Hawkins and Jacqui Hawkins (Walker Books, 1996)

Looking After My Pet Hamster (Looking After My Pet), David Alderton (Lorenz Books, 2002)

Looking After Your Hamster, Helen Piers (Frances Lincoln, 2002)

The Wild Side Of Pet Hamsters, Jo Waters (Raintree, 2005)

Useful addresses

Most countries have organizations and societies that work to protect animals from cruelty, and to help people learn how to care for the pets they live with properly.

UK
Royal Society for the Prevention
   of Cruelty to Animals (RSPCA)
Wilberforce Way
Southwater
Horsham
West Sussex
RH13 9RS
Tel: 0870 33 35 999
Fax: 0870 75 30 284

Australia
RSPCA Australia Inc.
PO Box 265
Deakin West ACT 2600
Tel.: 02 6282 8300
Fax: 02 6282 8311

Internet
There are hundreds of pet websites on the Internet. Here are a few that have information for young people.

You will find a lot of information about Syrian and dwarf hamsters at www.hamsterific.com. There are notes about cages, care, and health problems.

At this website you will see a lot of great pictures of other people's hamsters, and some instructions to make your own hamster toys! www.hamstercare.co.uk/

Disclaimer
All the Internet addresses (URLs) given in this book were valid at the time of going to press. However, due to the dynamic nature of the Internet, some addresses may have changed, or sites may have changed or ceased to exist since publication. While the author and Publishers regret any inconvenience this may cause readers, no responsibility for any such changes can be accepted by either the author or the Publishers.

Index